How to Draw
WILD
HORSES

Written by **Lisa Regan**, **Beckie Willams** and **Nicholas Forder**

Illustrated by **Nicholas Forder**

TOP THAT! **Kids**™

How to Draw
WILD HORSES

Everyone can draw something, whether it's a stick man, a swirly pattern, a detailed building plan, or a beautiful portrait. When you decide to 'learn' to draw, what you're really trying to do is draw something recognisable – either realistic, or fun like a cartoon. This book aims to teach you how to draw realistic-looking horses.

Before you can really learn to draw, you need to learn to look. If you want to draw wild horses, it's a good idea to take a trip to some stables with a sketch pad and pencil. Artists are very good at picking out the key characteristics of their subject (the thing they are drawing). You need to focus on the proportions of what you see – how long the horse's lower leg is in comparison to its upper leg, for example.

Start to observe how different colours work together to create different tones, and how light creates shadows and highlights, and changes the colours you see. The key to becoming a good artist is to look closely at what you intend to draw.

How to Draw

BASIC TOOLS

PENCILS

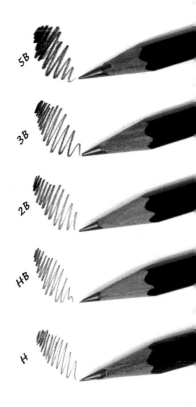

Drawing pencils are made up of a wooden case surrounding a graphite stick in the centre, which is what makes a mark on the paper. The graphite is mixed with clay; the more clay, the 'harder' the pencil. Letter H on a pencil stands for hard, and 2H or 3H and so on means they're harder still. These pencils leave less graphite on the paper, making a line which is lighter in tone. A letter B tells you how dark the line will be (sometimes referred to as the softness of the pencil). Again, 2B or 3B means the pencil is even softer. A letter F means that the pencil can be sharpened to a very fine point.

To copy the drawings in this book, it's best to have a selection of pencils. Try H, HB and 3B to start with. Draw soft outlines with your HB pencil and fill in more detail with your 3B and H pencils.

PAPER

Make sure you buy a sketch pad that isn't too big (you'll waste lots of white space around the edges and it's harder to carry around with you). Try to find paper that's white, instead of cream, and not see-through if you hold a sheet up to the light. Unless you're going to use watercolours as well as coloured pencils, you shouldn't need to buy expensive textured art paper.

SHARPENERS AND RUBBERS

You'll need a pencil sharpener, of course, but to get a very fine point on your pencil you'll also need sandpaper. The easiest way to do this is to borrow a nail file from an adult! There are lots of fancy erasers in the shops, but you want a plain-coloured artist's eraser. (The novelty ones in bright colours are no use for this kind of drawing.) You might also need a putty rubber which can be moulded into the right shape to shade areas of your drawing – good quality sticky putty works well for this.

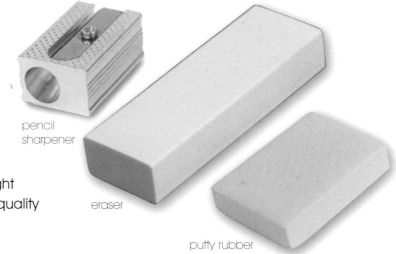

pencil sharpener

eraser

putty rubber

How to Draw

BASIC TECHNIQUES

This section explores some of the basic techniques you will need to develop if you are to successfully draw the horses in this book. Becoming familiar with your pencils and discovering what texture and lines they create and what they should be used for is central to being a good artist. Learn versatility: how to draw lightly and how to add strong details and shading. Try to see your subjects differently, breaking them down into shapes and studying their proportions.

USING YOUR PENCILS

Here is an example of how to use your pencils to re-create a realistic looking horse's face. Mastering the techniques required for this activity, which include drawing a soft outline, adding detail, shading and highlights, will set you in good stead for the rest of the book.

1 Use an HB pencil to lightly draw the basic outlines of the horse's head, as shown, above.

2 Using an HB pencil, start to add some basic shading and detail to your drawing. Make the softer outlines darker and add more depth to the contours and muscles in the face. Add the first layer of shadow to the underside of the horse's eye.

3 Continue to add depth to the drawing with further shading using a 2B pencil and for the darkest parts a 3B pencil. Notice where light reflects from the face and use your eraser to achieve white highlights in these places.

It's very easy to shade in an area of your drawing and then accidentally smudge it with your hand. One way to avoid this is to put a piece of paper under your hand while you are drawing.

SHADING TECHNIQUES

Don't be afraid to shade using your harder pencils. Just remember that harder pencil tones can't be rubbed out in the same way as your light pencil marks, if you make a mistake. Practise shading with different types of pencil and study other people's drawings – you'll see that they often use several different tones to create shadows, instead of just black.

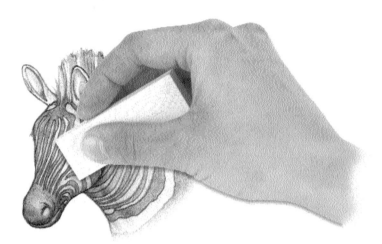

Use your fingertip to smudge areas for a very soft effect. Your putty rubber can lift pencil marks right off the page. Keep one corner of your ordinary eraser very sharp and angled so that you can use it like a pencil point. This is effective for adding white or pale highlights.

USING SHAPES

As you read this book you'll learn to see how creatures are made up of certain shapes. When you study an animal, check out all the proportions involved. Is the tail half the length of the body, or twice as long? Draw in these shapes and proportions very faintly at first so you can change them if necessary.

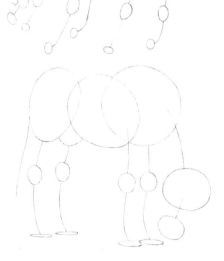

How to Draw

COLOURING EFFECTS

This section shows you how to develop the colouring techniques you will use throughout this book, and how to really bring your drawing to life. Colouring pencils can be used to create realistic looking tones, shadows and highlights. Learning to blend several different colours together will provide you with a wonderful way of capturing the true nature of horses' coats and the subtle shades within them.

APPLYING COLOUR

It is best to use ordinary colouring pencils to get to grips with the drawing techniques in this book. Begin by studying your chosen creature, or a photograph of it. Look carefully at how many different colours and shades give it the overall effect.

1 *Your first colour should be the lightest shade you see on the horse. Colour gently and evenly wherever you need this colour. Don't forget to miss areas if you need white highlights, or very dark areas with no pale shades.*

2 *Now gradually add darker colours to the drawing. These will start to form the shapes and contours of the creature's muscles and coat. Details such as these will gradually be built up as you draw.*

Deep Vermilion

Orange Chrome

Deep Cadmium

May Green

Emerald Green

Spectrum Blue

Prussian Blue

Light Violet

Imperial Purple

BLENDING COLOURS

You'll have to learn to study your subjects very carefully to get realistic colours. Many horses' coats have lots of subtle shades within them. You'll see that there's a huge difference between a horse with a brown coat with grey highlights, and one with a brown coat with red highlights. The colour chart (right) should give you a good idea of which colours blend together to create certain shades.

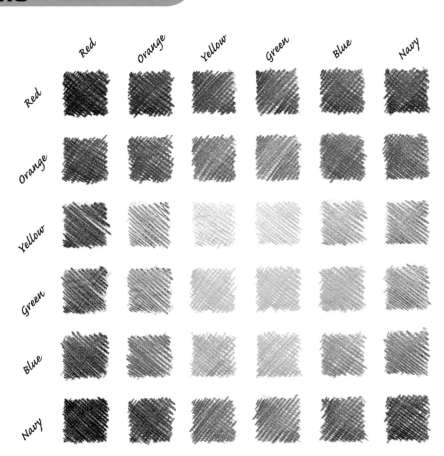

SHADOW AND LIGHT

After drawing the basic outline, look at your subject to see which parts are in shadow and which have light falling on them. Shadows and highlights are easy to spot in real life, but more difficult to capture on paper.

Highlights should be a paler version of the basic foundation colour. Don't just leave an area white – remove some colour with your eraser to leave a hint of what was there. Add brown or red, or yellow, to give a warm, or cold, effect.

Shadows should be built up carefully, adding more and more colour to the right areas. Think about how the light is being blocked to cast the shadow. Look carefully at how tones change, and how muscles are shaped, to add shadows to the right areas.

How to Draw
GRAZING HORSE

Horses have small stomachs so they need to eat for most of the day. They graze standing up, using their long necks to reach the short, young grasses. Horses need open spaces with lots of room to graze or they become unhappy and unhealthy. Horses actually use more energy lying down than standing up. They can lock their knees so that they can remain standing for long periods of time.

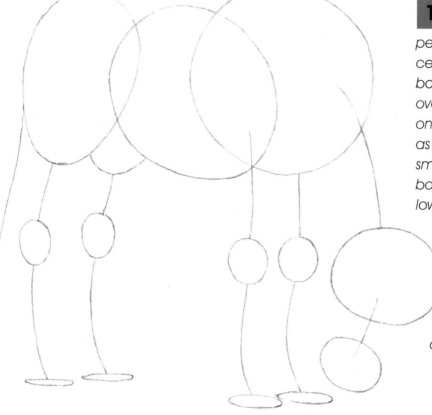

1 Start by sketching the skeleton with an HB pencil. Draw a large oval in the centre to create the main body. Now add two more ovals overlapping the main body: one at the front, the same size as the main body; and a smaller oval, pulled out at the bottom, at the back, for the lower body. Add two ovals for the head, and four ovals for the knees and join them to the body. Then draw four flat ovals for the hooves and join them to the knees. Draw a line for the tail at the back.

2 Now build on the skeleton by outlining and fleshing out the powerful body. Using ovals, add the shape of the muscles in the upper body and draw in the ankles. Use flowing lines to shape the overall outline of the horse, including its mane and tail.

Pay attention to the fullness and length of the mane and tail. These were especially thick and hardy because the horse lived in harsh conditions.

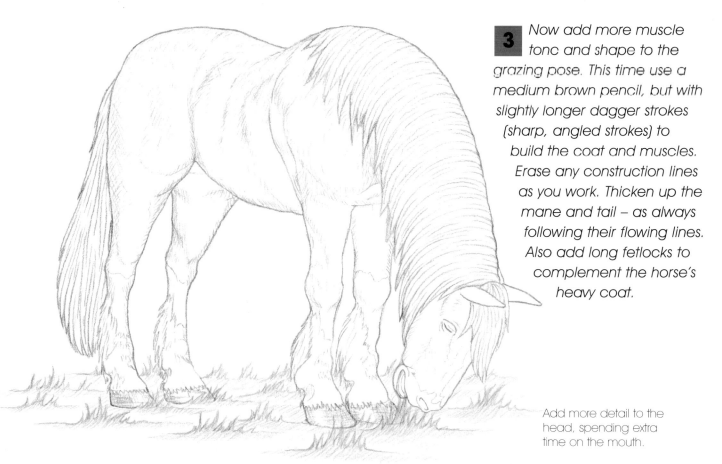

3 Now add more muscle tone and shape to the grazing pose. This time use a medium brown pencil, but with slightly longer dagger strokes (sharp, angled strokes) to build the coat and muscles. Erase any construction lines as you work. Thicken up the mane and tail – as always following their flowing lines. Also add long fetlocks to complement the horse's heavy coat.

Add more detail to the head, spending extra time on the mouth.

As the fetlocks are black and white, use a pale grey pencil to give them some shape. Blend the black and white fetlocks and brown legs together using short strokes for softness.

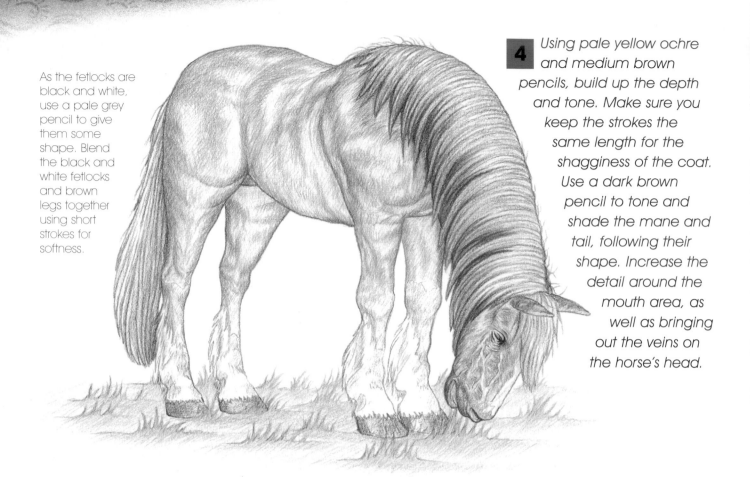

4 Using pale yellow ochre and medium brown pencils, build up the depth and tone. Make sure you keep the strokes the same length for the shagginess of the coat. Use a dark brown pencil to tone and shade the mane and tail, following their shape. Increase the detail around the mouth area, as well as bringing out the veins on the horse's head.

5 Using medium red brown, dark red brown and dark brown pencils, tone things down further on the coat to increase the depth of colour and shadow. Using pale grey and dark grey pencils develop the fetlocks and hooves. Continue with the shading until you are happy with the overall look. This time you should have a lovely drawing of an ancient, powerful, grazing horse.

How to Draw
REARING HORSE

A horse rears up when it is extremely frightened or when it is trying to show its dominance over another horse. By rising up on its hind legs the horse can appear bigger and stronger and use its front legs to kick. A rearing horse can be very dangerous and should only be calmed down and handled by an experienced trainer.

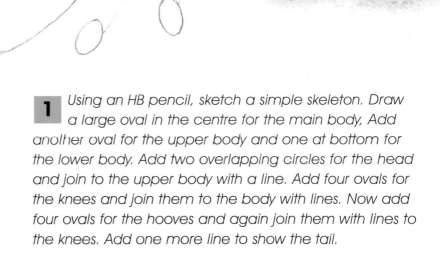

1 *Using an HB pencil, sketch a simple skeleton. Draw a large oval in the centre for the main body. Add another oval for the upper body and one at bottom for the lower body. Add two overlapping circles for the head and join to the upper body with a line. Add four ovals for the knees and join them to the body with lines. Now add four ovals for the hooves and again join them with lines to the knees. Add one more line to show the tail.*

2 Continue to add ovals and lines in the upper body to define the overall shape. Add four more ovals near the hooves to show the ankles. Now the fun really starts as you outline the shape using flowing lines including the mane and tail. Also add the eye, ears and mouth details to the head.

3 Add some simple muscle tone using a medium brown pencil. Use short strokes to follow the flow of the coat and muscles to build up the shape. Always make sure your strokes follow the coat and muscle direction. Erase any unnecessary construction lines. Now add more detail to the main facial features.

Use longer strokes to add more detail to the tail and mane.

4 Continue to add more depth and tone to the coat using brown and medium brown pencils. Spend more time building up the main features of the head and neck area. Use a pale grey and medium grey for the tail, mane and hooves. Follow this until you have an almost finished drawing, that's light in tone and colour.

5 Use a medium brown and darker brown to add more tone and depth to the overall coat and shadowy areas. Work on the details of the head. Take a medium grey and a dark grey to add further detail to the hooves, mane and tail. Continue in this way until you are happy with your horse.

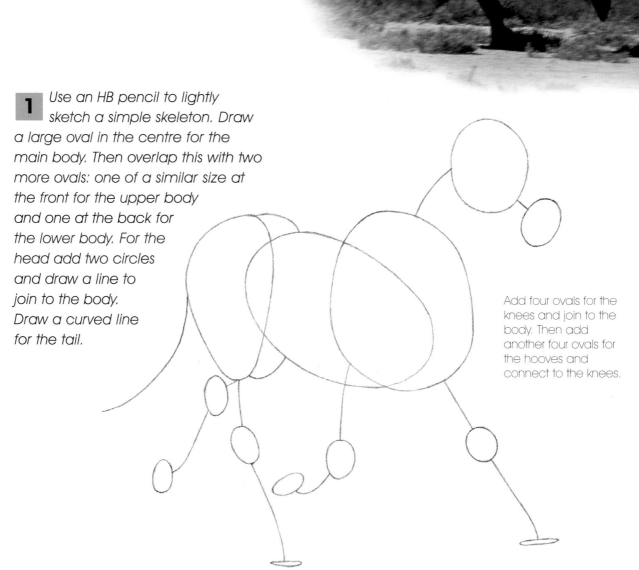

How to Draw
TROTTING HORSE

A trot is a fast walk. When horses trot their legs move diagonally in pairs, and only one hoof is ever touching the floor at a time. Each stride the horse takes makes a two-time rhythm with two beats. It is a natural gait which horses may perform in the wild.

1 *Use an HB pencil to lightly sketch a simple skeleton. Draw a large oval in the centre for the main body. Then overlap this with two more ovals: one of a similar size at the front for the upper body and one at the back for the lower body. For the head add two circles and draw a line to join to the body. Draw a curved line for the tail.*

Add four ovals for the knees and join to the body. Then add another four ovals for the hooves and connect to the knees.

Create movement in the mane and tail by keeping your pencil strokes long and curved backwards.

2 Develop the upper body by adding more ovals and lines for the muscle shapes. Add four ovals for the ankles between the knees and hooves. Using flowing lines, outline the shape of the horse, including the mane and tail.

3 Flesh out the muscle tone and add some texture to the coat using an HB pencil. Build up the shape of the coat and muscles with short strokes. Make sure your strokes follow the flow of the coat and the muscles. Now add more detail to the main facial features. Also shape the mane and tail with long strokes.

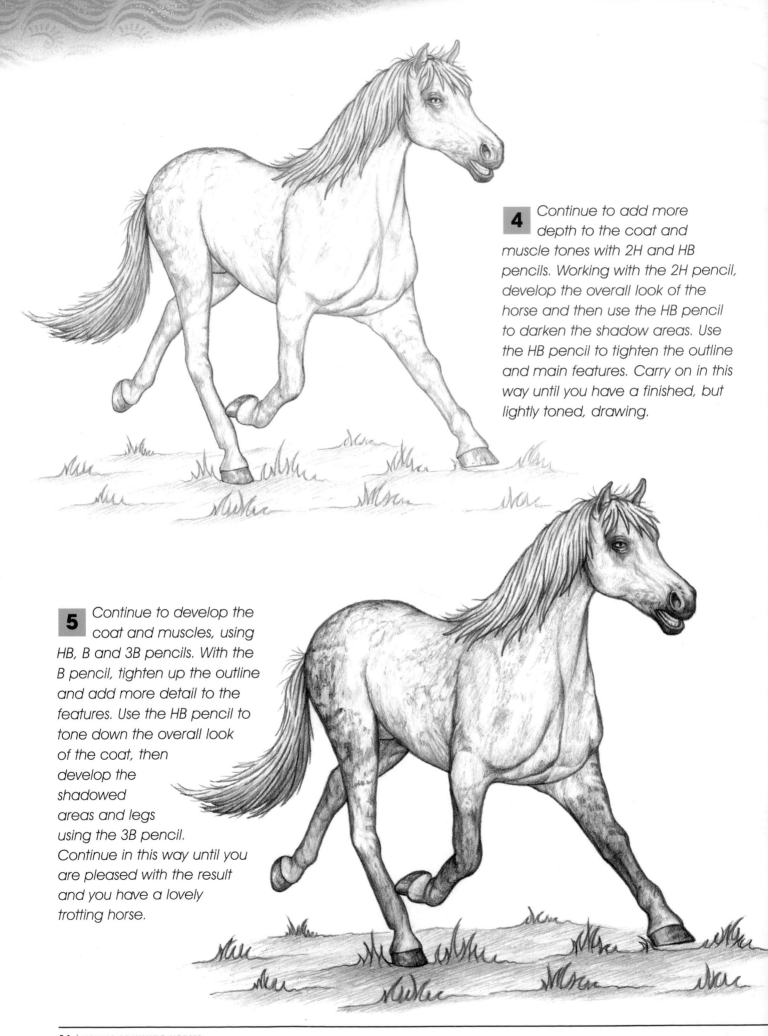

4 Continue to add more depth to the coat and muscle tones with 2H and HB pencils. Working with the 2H pencil, develop the overall look of the horse and then use the HB pencil to darken the shadow areas. Use the HB pencil to tighten the outline and main features. Carry on in this way until you have a finished, but lightly toned, drawing.

5 Continue to develop the coat and muscles, using HB, B and 3B pencils. With the B pencil, tighten up the outline and add more detail to the features. Use the HB pencil to tone down the overall look of the coat, then develop the shadowed areas and legs using the 3B pencil. Continue in this way until you are pleased with the result and you have a lovely trotting horse.

How to Draw

TARPAN

The tarpan is a prehistoric wild horse – even cave drawings have been found of them. Tarpans are a smoky grey colour with a dark mane and tail. They are small horses, but have thick necks and large heads with huge, powerful jaws.

Where do they live?

Although they have been extinct since the late 1800s, German zoologists have re-created them using genes from other breeds descended from the tarpan. Originally they lived across Europe, but today there are only 100 tarpan in the world and they all live in captivity.

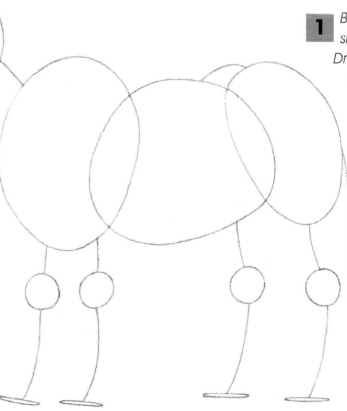

Add two circles for the large head, but not too far from the upper body as tarpan have a short, but muscular, neck.

1 Begin by sketching a skeleton with an HB pencil. Draw a large oval in the centre for the stocky main body, then add two more ovals, one of a similar size at the front for the strong, muscular, upper body and one at the back for the lower body. Now add four ovals for the knees then four for the hooves. Connect the hooves to the knees and then to the body. Finally, add a line at the back for the tail.

Draw the basic shapes of the mane and tail keeping the strokes long and loose for the rough appearance. Remember the tarpan lived a long time ago in harsh terrains and climates.

2 Using an HB pencil, add more lines to define the shape of the powerful muscles. Add four more ovals above the hooves for the ankles. Using flowing strokes, outline the stocky, strong, powerful shape. Finally, add the main features to the head.

3 Add some simple muscle tone using the HB pencil. Use medium length dagger strokes, following the flow of the coat and muscles, to get the shape. Erase any unnecessary construction lines as you work. Using longer dagger strokes, work on the mane and tail. Spend plenty of time detailing the main features of the head.

4 Continue to add more depth and tone to the coat using 2H and HB pencils. Go over the whole horse with the 2H pencil, following the flow of its shape with medium dagger strokes to increase the overall depth of tone. Now work on the darker areas and shadows with the HB pencil. Use it to tone down the mane and tail. Then tighten up the whole outline and main features, also with the HB pencil.

5 Add more depth and tone using HB, B and 3B pencils. Work all over the horse with the HB then the B pencil and finally use the 3B to tone down the shadows on the coat and the really dark areas. Take your B pencil now and carefully tighten up the outline and the main features.

Please take your time with the finishing details – it is worth it in the long run. Rushing will only spoil your drawing.

How to Draw

SHETLAND PONY

Shetland ponies are the oldest breed of horse in Britain. They are short, stocky ponies with thick, muscular legs and shaggy hair which protects them from the harsh weather of the Shetland Islands where they originated. Although they look small they are incredibly powerful and were once used to haul coal from mines.

Where do they live?

Although Shetland ponies were originally from the Shetland Islands, they were eventually exported to work in coal mines across Britain and America. They can now be found worldwide.

1 *Using an HB pencil, lightly sketch out a simple skeleton. Draw a large oval in the centre for the Shetland's barrel-shaped main body. Add two more ovals overlapping the main body for the large upper body and the lower body. Add four ovals for the knees, close to the body because the Shetland pony's legs are short but strong. Draw four more ovals for the hooves, again keeping them close to the knees. Add two more circles and join them with a line, for the small head, but keeping them close to the body. Add a long line for the tail at the back.*

Add the shape of the mane and tail using long strokes. These are very full, thick and shaggy – even more so for this pose as we are drawing this Shetland with a winter coat.

2 Now have some fun and see your Shetland come to life by outlining and fleshing her out. Using more ovals and lines in the upper body, define the powerful muscles. Add the main head features such as the eyes, ears and nostrils.

3 Now start building up the coat and muscle tone with a medium brown pencil. Use long dagger strokes, following the line of the coat and muscles, to develop the thick winter coat. make even longer strokes to thicken up the mane and tail. Go back to the head and spend some time working up the main features. Erase any unwanted construction lines as you progress.

4 Now add more depth and overall tone to the coat using pale brown, medium-red and brown pencils. Tone the mane and tail using pale yellow and yellow ochre pencils. Remember to keep your strokes long and follow the flow of the coat, mane and tail to keep the natural or unkept look of the horse.

5 Use pale brown, medium red brown and dark brown pencils to add depth and tone to the pony's coat and shadows. For the mane and tail, use pale yellow ochre and pale brown pencils to add tone. Use the pencils very sparingly to make it look like a rich golden colour rather than a dirty colour. Continue until you have a lovely Shetland pony in her winter coat.

How to Draw

DARTMOOR PONY

Dartmoor ponies have smooth, sloping shoulders and tiny ears. Although quite small, they are strong and very good at jumping. They are also fast and agile, and make excellent riding and competition horses.

Where do they live?

Dartmoor ponies originated on the wild moorland in south-western England. They are very rare in the wild now and are mostly bred in stud farms across Britain and in the United States.

Add two circles for the head and join to the upper body with a short line for the muscular neck. Add four ovals for the knees, then four more for the hooves.

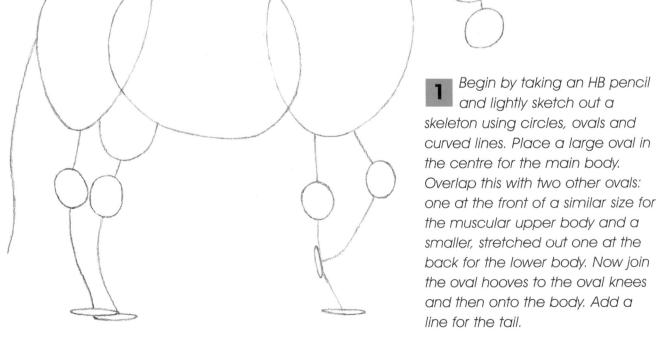

1 *Begin by taking an HB pencil and lightly sketch out a skeleton using circles, ovals and curved lines. Place a large oval in the centre for the main body. Overlap this with two other ovals: one at the front of a similar size for the muscular upper body and a smaller, stretched out one at the back for the lower body. Now join the oval hooves to the oval knees and then onto the body. Add a line for the tail.*

2 *Now you can have some fun outlining your pony and fleshing it out. Continue to add ovals and lines to the upper body and neck area to show the muscular shape. Add four ovals just above the hooves for the ankles; then using long, flowing strokes, outline the pony. Move on to the head and add its basic features.*

Finally take time to draw in long loose strokes for the mane and tail, which are unkempt and rough.

3 *Flesh out your Dartmoor pony some more and add simple muscle tone, using an HB pencil. Erase any construction lines as you work. Now spend a little time putting in details of the main features of the head. Next, move onto the mane and tail and add more detail using long dagger strokes.*

Use medium-long dagger strokes to follow the flow of the coat and muscles to build up the shape. Make sure you don't make the strokes too short and go with the flow of the shapes.

4 Use a 2H pencil to define the overall coat, remembering to keep those medium-length dagger strokes flowing with the coat. Next, work on the shadow areas with the HB pencil. Move onto the mane and tail and with the HB pencil add more depth of tone. Spend some time detailing out the head again and then tighten up the outline.

5 Using HB, B and 3B pencils add more tone and depth to the coat. Remember to work from lighter pencils to darker ones, rather than shading down with just a 3B pencil. This will help the coat look more natural in tone. Continue along these lines until you are happy with the look, then tighten up the outline and features with a B pencil. When you have finished, you should have a small, but strong, Dartmoor pony.

How to Draw

ZEBRA

Zebras are close relatives of the horse. They are recognisable from their stripes, which are unique to each individual animal. Zebras live in small groups but in the rainy season they are known to gather in massive herds of up to 10,000.

Where do they live?

Zebras live across the plains of Africa, mostly on the Serengetti-Mara plain in the east of the continent.

All of the ovals and circles are much larger than previously drawn because zebras are much stockier than modern wild horses.

1 Start by using an HB pencil to sketch a simple skeleton. Draw a large oval for the main body in the centre. Overlap this with two more ovals, one at the front for the upper body and one at the back for the lower body. For the head, add two circles and join them to the body. Now add four ovals for the knees and then four for the hooves. Join the hooves to the knees and then on to the body. Finally, add a line at the back for the tail.

Pay particular attention to the ears, as zebras have large, upright ears which they use to listen for predators in the wild.

2 Taking your HB pencil outline and flesh out your zebra skeleton. Add more ovals and lines to the upper body to develop the strong, muscular shape. Add four more ovals just above the hooves for the ankles. Move on to the head and add the main facial features. Next, add the very distinctive upright mane and the tail. Now, using long, flowing strokes, outline the whole animal.

3 With the HB pencil, use short strokes to add some basic muscle tone. First though, add the distinctive stripes of the zebra, which may allow it to blend into the herd to avoid the unwanted gaze of predators. Add further muscle tone, remembering to follow the flow of the coat and muscles. Erase any unnecessary construction lines as you go. Move to the head and spend time detailing out the features. Now progress to the mane and tail and put in their details.

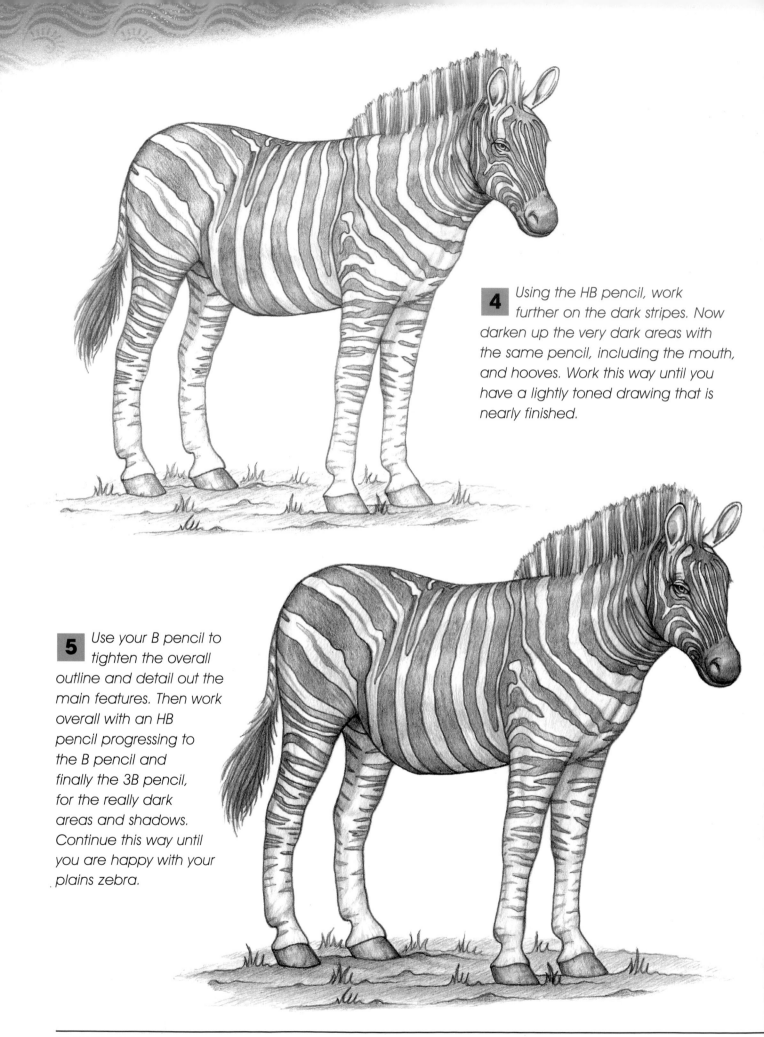

4 Using the HB pencil, work further on the dark stripes. Now darken up the very dark areas with the same pencil, including the mouth, and hooves. Work this way until you have a lightly toned drawing that is nearly finished.

5 Use your B pencil to tighten the overall outline and detail out the main features. Then work overall with an HB pencil progressing to the B pencil and finally the 3B pencil, for the really dark areas and shadows. Continue this way until you are happy with your plains zebra.

How to Draw

HERDS

Horses naturally live and travel together in groups called herds. They are very sociable animals and extremely protective of each other. Being in herds protects the horses and makes them stronger against attackers. They make intense friendships that they never forget and are not easily separated from others in their herd or family.

There is always a dominant horse in a herd: called the alpha. Unlike most animals, an alpha horse is not determined by strength or power. The oldest, most experienced, horse is naturally appointed as the leader of the herd.

1 *To begin drawing the herd of wild horses, sketch out their simple skeletons, using a 2H pencil. This time, though, draw only what you see so as not to over complicate the lines more. You should be familiar with how to build up the shapes with circles and ovals by now. Just take your time and add the simple skeleton shapes one by one.*

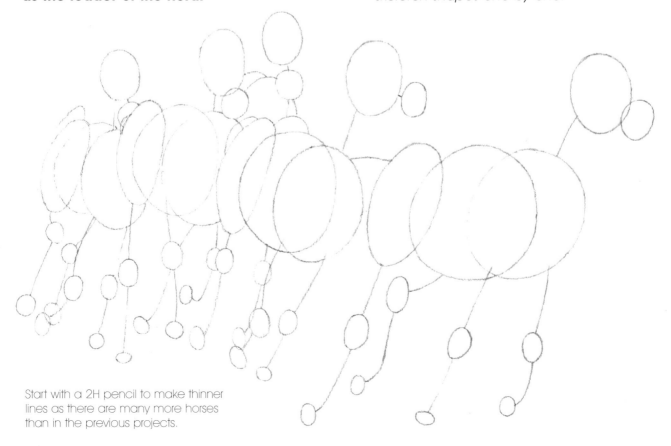

Start with a 2H pencil to make thinner lines as there are many more horses than in the previous projects.

2 Next, outline and flesh out each of the horses. Add ovals and lines to develop their upper body muscle tones. Add ovals for the ankles, but only the ones you can see. Add all the basic features to each head. Finally, use long, flowing strokes to add more shape to the horses. Remember to keep them flowing to achieve that dynamic look of movement.

For the manes and tails make sure you get the sense of motion and speed by having them flow backwards.

3 Using a 2H pencil, add some basic muscle tones with short strokes. Following the flow of the coats as you add them. Erase any unwanted construction lines as you work, then spend some time adding detail to the horses' main features, flowing manes and tails. It is better to do this slowly and carefully rather than rush it and mess it up. Finally tighten up the outline of the herd with a B pencil.

This stage will take some time, so if you want to have a break leave the drawing for a while and then come back to it.

4 Add more depth and tone to the herd using your 2H and HB pencils. Tone the coats down with the 2H pencil, then take the HB pencil and add tone to the areas in shadow. Now use the HB pencil to tone down the manes and tails. Move on to the head and add more detail to the features. Have a break and then go back and tighten up the outlines with your HB pencil.

5 As you did on the previous projects, start with an HB pencil and move on to a 3B pencil for the really dark areas toning down the horses' coats. Again, this will take some time so take breaks. Once you are happy with the overall tone, outline each horse and detail out the main features with your B pencil. Continue this way until you are happy and you have a herd of galloping wild horses.

How to Draw

FOALS

Most foals are born in the spring, during the night-time. A foal's legs are already almost fully grown when it is born. Although they can stand after just a couple of hours, it does make it hard for them to graze and the gangly foals have to rely on their mother's milk for several months.

It's hard to tell what colour a foal will be when it is fully grown. They change colour regularly and only settle down when the horse is about two years old. A horse is fully grown at the age of four years.

1 *To start, sketch out the simple skeleton using an HB pencil. Draw a medium oval in the centre for the foal's main body, then towards the front add an oval stretched out on the vertical for the upper body, and at the back add another smaller oval for the lower body. Now add two circles for the foal's head, only slightly overlapping. Draw four ovals for the knees adding lines to connect to body. Then draw four ovals for the hooves and join them to knees.*

Remember to draw the skeleton of the legs, even if they are behind, because this will help the natural shape of the foal later.

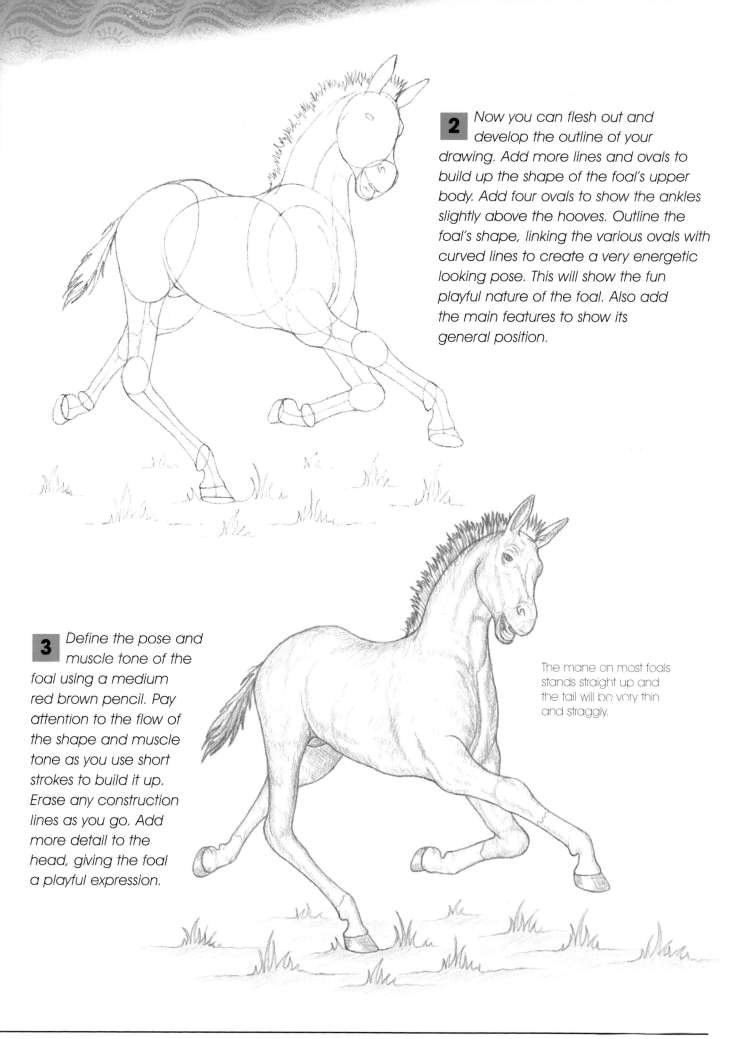

2 Now you can flesh out and develop the outline of your drawing. Add more lines and ovals to build up the shape of the foal's upper body. Add four ovals to show the ankles slightly above the hooves. Outline the foal's shape, linking the various ovals with curved lines to create a very energetic looking pose. This will show the fun playful nature of the foal. Also add the main features to show its general position.

3 Define the pose and muscle tone of the foal using a medium red brown pencil. Pay attention to the flow of the shape and muscle tone as you use short strokes to build it up. Erase any construction lines as you go. Add more detail to the head, giving the foal a playful expression.

The mane on most foals stands straight up and the tail will be very thin and straggly.

4 Continue to add depth and tone to the foal's coat using pale yellow ochre, medium red brown, dark brown and pale grey pencils. To fade between the two colours in the coat, overlap some of the pale grey into the brown area and some of the yellow ochre into the white. Again, spend plenty of time on the head developing the expression of the foal. Build up the overall colour and tone to an almost finished, but light, tone. Remember to follow the shape and muscle tone of the horse.

Because the underbody and legs of the foal are white, use the pale grey pencil to tone in this area.

5 Following on from step 4 using medium red brown, dark red brown, dark brown, pale grey and dark grey pencils to build up the colour of the foal's coat increasing the depth and tone in the shadow areas. Detail out the head and hooves with darker tones and sharp lines to show the features. Continue in this way until you are happy with your carefree, playful foal.

How to Draw

MUSTANGS

Mustangs are wild horses from North America. They are a mixture of lots of different breeds of horses brought over by colonists in the 1800s and 1900s; a combination of Spanish, French and British working and military horses. Because of this, mustangs come in every colour possible. They can be tamed and make excellent riding horses, especially over long distances.

Where do they live?
Mustangs are found across the plains of the Western United States.

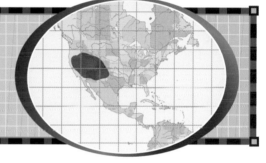

1 To start your mustang, lightly sketch his skeleton using an HB pencil. Add an oval in the centre for the main body, overlapping at the front a similar sized one for the upper body. At the back draw a squashed oval for the lower body. For the head, add two circles not that far from the body as mustangs have a short neck and their face is long. Add a flowing line at the back for the tail.

Draw four ovals for the knees a little further from the body as mustangs are known for their strong legs. Also add four ovals for the hooves and join them to the knees and then on to the body.

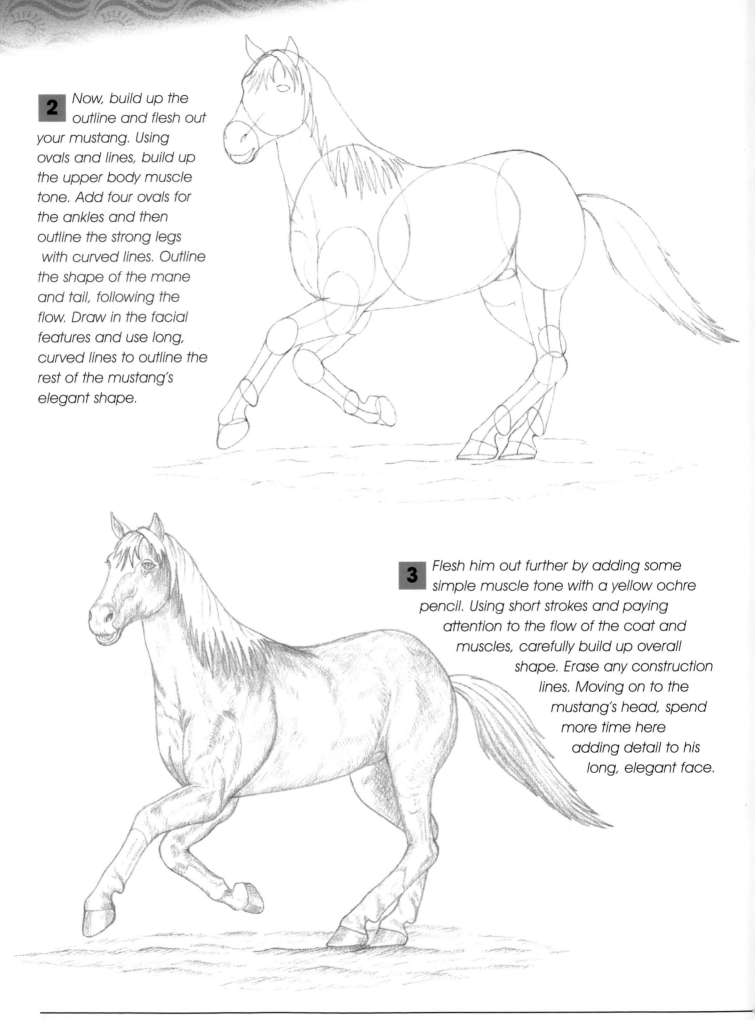

2 Now, build up the outline and flesh out your mustang. Using ovals and lines, build up the upper body muscle tone. Add four ovals for the ankles and then outline the strong legs with curved lines. Outline the shape of the mane and tail, following the flow. Draw in the facial features and use long, curved lines to outline the rest of the mustang's elegant shape.

3 Flesh him out further by adding some simple muscle tone with a yellow ochre pencil. Using short strokes and paying attention to the flow of the coat and muscles, carefully build up overall shape. Erase any construction lines. Moving on to the mustang's head, spend more time here adding detail to his long, elegant face.

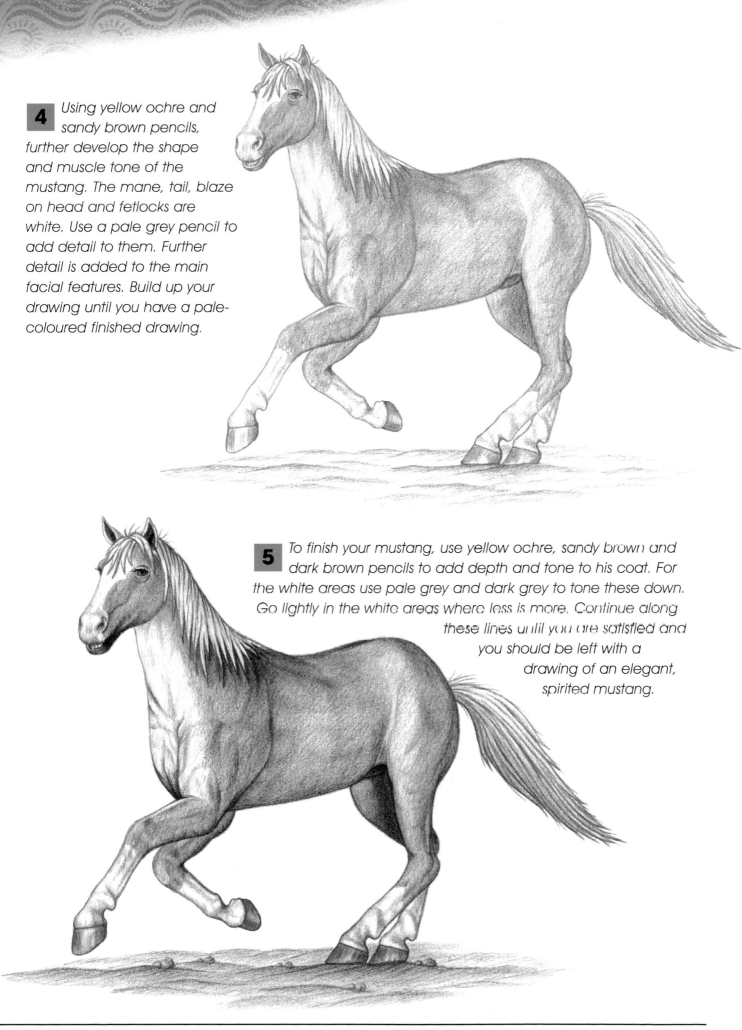

4 Using yellow ochre and sandy brown pencils, further develop the shape and muscle tone of the mustang. The mane, tail, blaze on head and fetlocks are white. Use a pale grey pencil to add detail to them. Further detail is added to the main facial features. Build up your drawing until you have a pale-coloured finished drawing.

5 To finish your mustang, use yellow ochre, sandy brown and dark brown pencils to add depth and tone to his coat. For the white areas use pale grey and dark grey to tone these down. Go lightly in the white areas where less is more. Continue along these lines until you are satisfied and you should be left with a drawing of an elegant, spirited mustang.

PLIOHIPPUS

The pliohippus was a prehistoric ancestor of the modern horse. It appeared around five million years ago and was more like the modern horse than earlier species. The pliohippus also had strong legs and scientists believe that they were very large and moved very quickly.

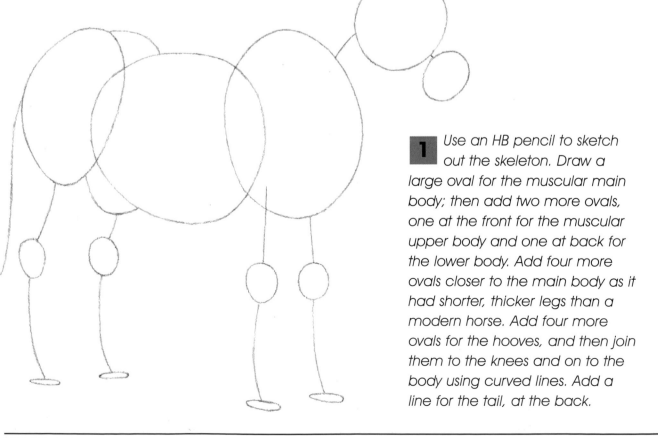

1 *Use an HB pencil to sketch out the skeleton. Draw a large oval for the muscular main body; then add two more ovals, one at the front for the muscular upper body and one at back for the lower body. Add four more ovals closer to the main body as it had shorter, thicker legs than a modern horse. Add four more ovals for the hooves, and then join them to the knees and on to the body using curved lines. Add a line for the tail, at the back.*

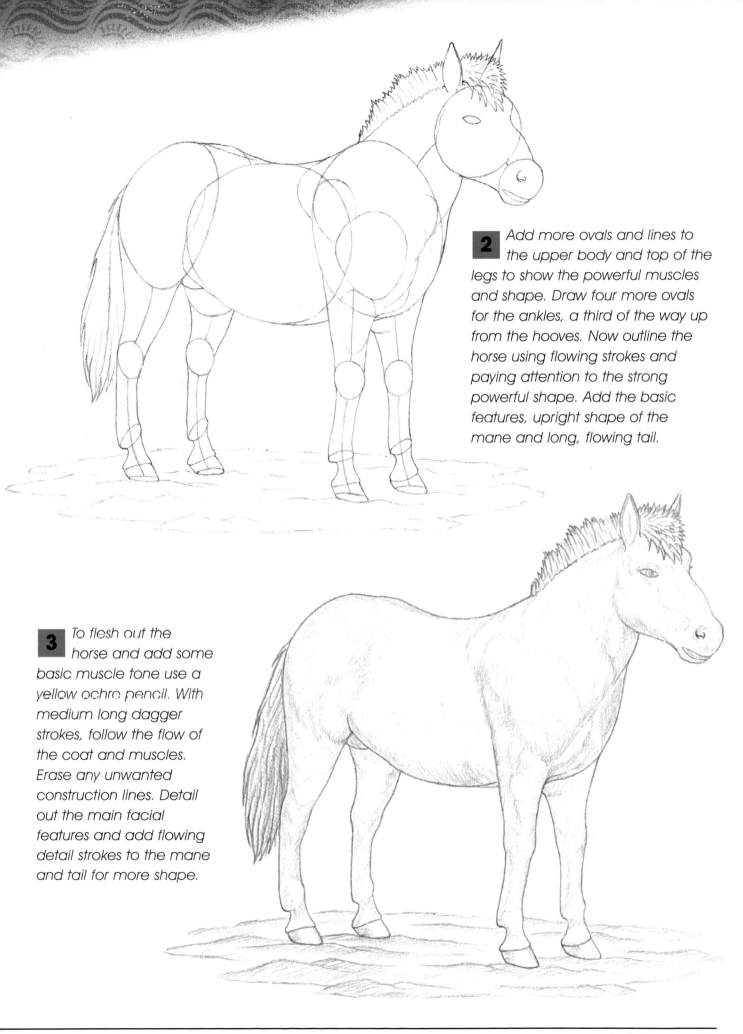

2 Add more ovals and lines to the upper body and top of the legs to show the powerful muscles and shape. Draw four more ovals for the ankles, a third of the way up from the hooves. Now outline the horse using flowing strokes and paying attention to the strong powerful shape. Add the basic features, upright shape of the mane and long, flowing tail.

3 To flesh out the horse and add some basic muscle tone use a yellow ochre pencil. With medium long dagger strokes, follow the flow of the coat and muscles. Erase any unwanted construction lines. Detail out the main facial features and add flowing detail strokes to the mane and tail for more shape.

4 Continue to add depth and tone to the horse's coat using yellow ochre, pale red brown and medium red brown pencils. For the underbody, add some pale grey pencil as this is white there, but cast in shadow. From the knees down, add some tone using a medium grey pencil. Also use this to darken the mane and the tail, and add detail to the eyes and the mouth.

5 Use medium brown and dark brown pencils to darken the coat and shadows. Use medium-grey and dark grey pencils to tone down the mane and tail. As always, follow the flow of the coat and keep the dagger strokes medium in length. Continue in this way until you are happy and you should see a finished pliohippus drawing.

How to Draw

ARABIAN

The world's oldest and most influential pure bred is the Arabian. It is descended, it is believed, from Asiatic wild stock that ran wild in the desert lands of the Middle East as long ago as 5000 BC. The dished face, great muscular strength, outstanding eyesight and hearing, courage, intelligence and stamina make this breed very special indeed. Arabians stand 14 to 15 hands tall.

Where do they live?

It is thought that Arabian horses originated in northern Syria and southern Turkey. Others suggest that they come from the southwestern part of Arabia. Today they are found throughout the world.

1 *Begin by taking an HB pencil and lightly sketch out a simple skeleton using circles, ovals and curved lines. Draw a large oval in the centre for the main body, overlap this with two other ovals. One at the front, in a similar size for the muscular upper body and a smaller, stretched out one at the back for the lower body. Now join the hooves to the knees and then to the body. Add a line down from the back for the tail.*

Add two circles for the head and join to the upper body with a line for the muscular neck. Add four ovals for the knees, then four more for the hooves.

2 *Now have some fun outlining the Arabian horse and fleshing it out. Continue to add ovals and lines to the upper body and neck area for the muscular shape. Next, move to the head and add the basic features.*

Spend some time to use long, loose strokes to add to the mane and tail.

3 *Flesh out the Arabian stallion more and add some simple muscle tone using a medium red brown pencil. Erase any construction lines now or as you work through, then spend a little time adding detail to the main features of the head. Move on to the mane and tail now and add some more detail with brown, grey and black pencils.*

Use medium-length dagger strokes to follow the flow of the horse's coat and muscles to build up the shape. Make sure you keep the strokes medium length and go with the flow of the shape.

4 Use a pale grey pencil to work up the overall coat, remembering to keep the medium-length dagger strokes flowing with the coat. Next, work in the shadow areas with an dark grey pencil. Move on to the mane and tail with the dark grey and brown pencils and add more depth of tone. Spend some time detailing out the head again and finally tighten up the outline with a dark grey pencil.

5 Using pale grey, dark grey and yellow pencils, add more tone and depth to the coat, mane and tail. Remember to work from lighter pencils to darker ones as this will help the coat to look more natural in tone rather than shading down with just a single pencil.

6 Continue to add more tones to the coat until you are happy with the overall look, then tighten up the horse's outline and features with a black pencil. When you have finished this you should see a majestic Arabian stallion.

How to Draw

MASTERCLASS DRAWINGS

Every artist starts as a beginner. The difference between a poor artist and a good one is a matter of observation, practice, and learning from other artworks. In the same way, every picture starts as a basic sketch. These pages will show you how to compose a drawing, and how to learn to look at things to see them as they really are.

OBSERVATION AND SKETCHING

The best way to learn how horses look is to take a sketch book to your local stables, and practice doing rough sketches of the horses you see. Study the way their bodies are put together and the varying textures of their coats.

Draw the rough outline first, using the simple shapes that you have learned to capture the proportions of the creature. Add more detail to your sketch to pinpoint where the main features are. If you're sketching roughs, make sure that you have enough detail to complete your picture.

Horses love to run around, so you'll have to watch them very closely to capture their main body shapes.

When you're doing your sketch, make some colour notes as you go along, or use coloured pencils in small areas to remind you of the colour differences. Your main sketching tool, however, is always your pencil.

1 *Make sketch notes of anything you find interesting or unusual about the animals. Maybe you have never noticed how playful and carefree the foal seems, or how it likes to stand close to its mother, for example.*

2 *Draw in some colour detail to remind yourself of the different tones that appear on the creature. What you leave off is as important as the marks you make on the paper. Look at this sketch (right). There is very little colour or pencil work at all in the highlights – the areas which are catching the most light.*

3 *Finally, the sketches and notes you make earlier should help you to create an acurate, and more detailed, picture when you begin your actual drawing.*

BACK AT HOME

With your sketches in front of you, you can decide in which position you want to draw your chosen animal. Don't panic if you have left some vital detail off your sketch. Photographs can be really helpful to fill in any gaps. Look in reference books and you should find examples. They will help you to study colours, textures and any other details your basic sketches may be lacking.

1 *Photographs can be a good way to start sketching. Try to see the hidden shapes, as shown in the step-by-steps earlier in this book. Learn to take the leap from looking at your animal, directly to sketching their main body shape, without having to draw the basic shapes.*

2 *Use photos when you're drawing to check that you have the right shades and hues. It's a great way to really focus in on some of the creature's finer details.*

SETTING THE SCENE

You may be happy with your foal on its own, but the chances are you'll want to add something else in the background. Experiment with different styles. Some pictures look great just with other animals behind them, others are better suited to a natural background such as a grassy valley.

In this example, the foal is joined by its mother. They have both been set against a simple background of trees and mountains. The context suggests that the horses are wild and free in their natural habitat.

You should study the background as you draw, just the way you've learnt to do with your horses. Look carefully at the areas of light and shadow. Notice the way that tones are more distinct in the foreground and fainter the further back you go.

WHEN IS A DRAWING FINISHED?

Don't overwork your pictures. Learn to recognise when you've done enough to create impact, without making your picture too busy or crowded. It's also important to learn that you can stop when you've had enough. Drawing is done for pleasure, so you shouldn't have to keep working at it until you're fed up. Having said that, it's quite likely that you'll get engrossed in your work and never want to stop!